A PRIMER ON ADLERIAN PSYCHOLOGY

A PRIMER ON ADLERIAN PSYCHOLOGY

*Behavior Management Techniques
for Young Children*

DR. ALEX L. CHEW, ED.D.

HUMANICS

*Humanics Trade
www.humanicspub.com*

HUMANICS

A Primer on Adlerian Psychology
A Humanics Publication

Published simultaneously in the United States, Canada, and the United Kingdom

Humanics Trade Publications are an imprint of and published by Humanics Publishing Group, a division of Brumby Holdings, Inc. Its trademark, consisting of the words "Humanics Trade" and the portrayal of a Pegasus, is registered in the U.S. Patent and Trademarks Office and in other countries.
Brumby Holdings, 12 South Dixie Hwy, Lake Worth, FL 33460

Printed in the United States of American and the United Kingdom

ISBN (Paperback): 0-89334-271-8
ISBN (Hardcover): 0-89334-272-6

DEDICATION AND ACKNOWLEDGEMENTS

This book is dedicated to my young friend Charles M. "Mitch" Warnock, Jr. Mitch's courage, determination and exceptional character have been an inspiration to me as it has to all that know and love him.

The contributions of Harriet H. Langford in the development of this book are gratefully acknowledged. Harriet, one of my former graduate students, is currently a school counselor in the Glynn County (Georgia) Public Schools.

About the Author

Dr. Alexander L. Chew, Ed.D. is Professor of Educational Psychology and Counseling and a member of the Graduate Faculty at Georgia Southern University, Statesboro, Georgia. He holds graduate degrees from the University of Georgia, Georgia Southern University, and the University of Mississippi, where he completed his Doctorate in Educational Psychology.

Dr. Chew holds doctoral level certification from the Georgia Department of Education in School Psychology, Counseling, and Administration and Supervision. He is also a Licensed Professional Counselor. Before joining the Georgia Southern University faculty in 1979, Dr. Chew was employed twelve years in public education. He has worked as a classroom teacher, school counselor, school psychologist, and as a school administrator.

Dr. Chew holds memberships in Phi Delta Kappa, a national honor society for professional educators, Phi Kappa Phi, a national academic honor society, and Chi Sigma Iota, a counseling academic and professional honor society international. He is a member of several professional divisions of the American Counseling association and the Licensed Professional Counselors Association of Georgia, having served on the latter's Board of Directors from 1992-1998. In 1991 he received the prestigious Georgia Southern University Award for excellence in Research. Dr. Chew has presented more than 150 professional papers and/or workshops, many concerning the psychoeducational evaluation of young children. He is probably best known nationally as the author and research developer of the *Lollipop Test: A Diagnostic Screening Test of School Readiness-Revised.*

Additional Publications by Dr. Chew
and Published by Humanics Publishing Group are:

The Lollipop Test: A Diagnostic Test of School Readiness-Revised
(1997)

PREFACE

Alfred Adler was born in 1870 in Vienna. He was the second son in a family of six children. His father was a middle-class Jewish merchant and his mother a housewife. In his early childhood he suffered from poor health, but as he grew older his health improved. His interest in medicine, which arose at an early age, led to a medical degree at the prestigious University of Vienna in 1895. In 1897 he married a classmate, a Russian woman from Moscow, and they had four children. Two of these, Dr. Kurt Adler and Dr. Alexandra Adler, became practicing psychotherapists in New York.

Adler specialized in ophthalmology, and then, after a period of practice in general medicine, he became a psychiatrist. Some feel that there may be some relationship between his early practice as an eye specialist and the many perceptual implications in his psychological theory. In 1902 Sigmund Freud invited Adler to become a member of his weekly discussion group. This group developed into The Vienna Psychoanalytic Society, of which Adler became president in 1910. However, Adler soon began to develop ideas that were at variance with those of Freud and others in the Society. When these difference became acute, he resigned as president in 1911. It should be noted that contrary to popular notion, Adler was not a disciple of Freud's; he was a colleague. After he terminated his ties with psychoanalysis, Adler devoted himself to developing his own system of thought. In 1912 The Society for Individual Psychology was born, and counted among its members a number of those who had belonged to Freud's Vienna Society. During World War I, Adler served as a physician in the Austrian army, and after the war he became interested in child guidance and established the first guidance clinics in connection with the Viennese school system. At these child-guidance centers, Adler demonstrated his techniques (an instructional idea that had never been used before that time) in front of audiences of professionals.

In 1926 Adler made his first lecture tour in the United States. After that his visits became more and more frequent, and eventually in 1935 he fled Europe and settled in the United States, where he continued his practice as a psychiatrist and served as Professor of Medical Psychology at the Long Island College of Medicine. Adler was a prolific writer and indefatigable lecturer. Adler published more than three hundred books and was considered "a man ahead of his times." In the autocratic era of the 1920's, Adler was writing and lecturing on such topics as juvenile delinquency, marriage counseling, masculine dominance, women's equality, children's toys, continuing education, and school reform. In 1923 Adler wrote on what he called "neurotic hunger strike." He stated that "the fear of eating begins as a rule at the age of seventeen and almost always with girls. Its adoption is generally followed by a rapid decrease in weight. The goal to be inferred from the whole attitude of the patient, is the rejection of the woman's role." Today we call this "anorexia nervosa."

Adler died in Aberdeen Scotland in 1937 while on a lecture tour. Fortunately, he had students and disciples who carried on his work. One of them was Rudolf Dreikurs, who settled in Chicago and was instrumental in founding the Alfred Adler Institute there. Dreikurs nurtured the growth of Adlerian Psychology in the United States until his death in 1971. The resurgence of the Adlerian school after the death of Adler was an uphill effort. However, men such as Dreikurs persevered, and in 1952 The American Society of Adlerian Psychology was founded. Several journals appeared; the two major American ones are *The Journal of Individual Psychology*, and *The Individual Psychologist*. Incorporation of Adlerian tenets and ideas is seen in many current psychotherapies, such as Ellis' Rational-Emotive, Glasser's Reality Therapy, Berne's Transactional Analysis, Sartre's Existential Psychoanalysis, Frankel's Logotherapy, Perl's Gestalt, and Roger's Client-Centered. All of this gives testimony to the renaissance of Adlerian Individual Psychology.

Adlerian Psychology has experienced a tremendous resurgence in the past 15 to 20 years. Close scrutiny will reveal that many of the more contemporary counseling therapies, i.e., Reality Therapy, Rational-Emotive Therapy, Transactional Analysis, and even Person Centered Therapy have all borrowed heavily from the basic tenets of Adlerian Psychology. In an attempt to integrate some of these extensive resources, this three-part primer was developed.

My graduated students have often reflected that learning counseling theory is one thing, but applying it to "real life" situations is sometimes more difficult. Therefore, in this book an attempt has been made to create a balance between theory and practical application.

It is hoped that this book will serve as a resource for both counseling and consultation activities. Elementary school counselors and psychologists may find many of the theoretical tenets and their practical applications helpful when making suggestions to teachers and parents concerning behavior management and/or discipline solutions. Similarly, parents of young children may be able to identify with some of the examples of behavior problems, their solutions, and apply them to home situations.

Regardless of the motivation of the reader—school counselor, parent, or graduate student—it is hoped that this book will create an interest and desire to further explore the procedures, techniques and great variety of resources that Adlerian Psychology has to offer to anyone working with young children.

TABLE OF CONTENTS

PART I

---

*An Overview of
Adlerian Psychology*

INTRODUCTION

Adlerian psychology has come to be recognized as the precursor to many current schools of psychological thought, including Eric Berne's Transactional Analysis, Albert Ellis' Rational-Emotive Therapy, and William Glasser's Reality Therapy. Additionally, Rudolph Reikurs' many contributions to Adlerian theory in the United States became known as Individual Psychology. One of Dreikurs' most widely utilized contributions was his understanding of children's "four goals of misbehavior" (Dinkmeyer & Dinkmeyer, 1983; Mosak, 1984). These four goals of misbehavior are explained in considerable detail in Part II of this book. Therefore, it appeared reasonable that a discussion of Adlerian psychology would serve as a useful and practical introduction to many of the concepts detailed in other sections of this book.

Part I of this monograph is divided into four main sections: (1) theoretical foundations of Adlerian psychology, which includes a review of basic concepts or tenets; (2) the development of personality, including a comprehensive discussion of birth order; (3) the development of the life styles; and (4) a brief discussion of selected applications of Adlerian psychology in educational settings.

Theoretical Foundations of Adlerian Psychology

Definition and Overview

Adlerian Psychology, or Individual Psychology, was developed by Alfred Adler in 1911 after his split with Freud. It is based on the assumption that people are unique, social, decision making beings whose actions and psychological movements have a purpose and a goal. Each person is seen as an indivisible being, within a social setting, with a capacity to decide and choose (Dinkmeyer, Pew & Dinkmeyer, 1979).

Others describe Individual Psychology as subjectivistic, phenomenological, and cognitive (Hansen, Warner & Smith, 1980). They maintain that it is subjectivistic in that it stresses the importance of studying behavior from the perspective of the individual; it is phenomenological in that it stresses dealing with individual's total perceptual field; and it is cognitive-oriented in that it asserts that thought processes control individuals' actions.

Individual Psychology gets its name form the basic concept of holism, that the person is Individuum — that is to say, an indivisible unit. Individual Psychology is really a social psychology in that it stresses that the individual is meaningless except in social terms, and that the person operates within a social setting (Manaster & Corsini, 1981). To Alfred Alder, Individual Psychology was more than just a compilation and interpretation of mental processes and behavior; it was a philosophy of life based on social living. Adler (1927) maintained that "no adequate man can grow up without cultivating a deep sense of his fellowship in humanity and practicing the art of being a human being" (p. 32).

Adlerians hold an optimistic point of view. They see the individual as central, intact, integrated, and in control of the self. They view life as an ongoing process and believe that people are striving for success which manifests itself in their unique goals, which are fictions they have developed (Manaster & Corsini, 1982). This optimistic psychology has wide applications through many activities in all areas of life, e.g., child guidance centers, parent training centers, schools, individual and group psychotherapy, and in the counseling of school children. As previously mentioned, certain techniques derived from Adlerian Psychology have enjoyed wide acceptance when dealing with children's behavior problems, which explains the appropriateness of this book's subtitle.

Basic Concepts

Adlerians view each person, even the youngest child in the family, as an individual, with the creative capacities to decide and choose. The actions of each person are purposeful, indivisible, and socially based. The following basic assumptions, as outlined in Dinkmeyer and Dinkmeyer (1983), Manaster and Corsini (1982(, and Dinkmeyer et al, (1979), best describe Adlerian theory.

1. All Behavior has Social Meaning

One of the basic premises of Adlerian theory is that we are primarily social beings and that our behavior occurs in a social context. A child is born into an environment with which he must engage in reciprocal relations. In fact, interaction with others is a continuous, life-long process. It begins in infancy when we are entirely dependent on others for our very survival. Later we need to cooperate with others in order to realize our goals and function fully.

Life Tasks is an Adlerian term used to describe a person's major goals or social needs. Adler believed that throughout life all of us must meet three major life tasks, which he defined as society, work, and sex.

Dreikurs uses slightly different terminology, referring to the tasks as work, friends, and love. He adds a fourth life task, "getting along with oneself," and a fifth existential task, "finding meaning to one's life."

Feeling of Belonging. A corollary of this first premise is that Individual Psychology is an interpersonal psychology. Transcending interpersonal transactions is the development of the feeling of belonging, the feeling of being a part of a larger social order. Children decide which groups are important to them and strive to gain acceptance. Many of the anxieties experienced by children stem from the fear that they will not be accepted by the group they seek to join; e.g., their siblings in the family or their peer group in the neighborhood or school. when a child's sense of belonging remains unfulfilled, the result is anxiety and unhappiness.

Each child is constantly faced with opportunities to interact with other children and adults. In the schools, teachers can use the natural social environment of the classroom to create situations that utilize the need to belong. Questions that teachers and counselors might explore, such as "Does the child get along well with classmates?" and "How does she get along with siblings and parents?" are clues to the social context or meaning of a child's behaviors.

2. Personality has Unity and Pattern

Adlerian psychology rejects reductionism in favor of holism. The person is seen as a dynamic, unified organism moving through life in definite patterns towards a goal. Fragmenting the personality by casual or analytical explanations denies this wholeness.

The word individual in Individual Psychology does not mean the opposite of "social" or "group." Individual psychology is not a psychology of individuals as opposed to groups of people. The term individuell in German has the connotation of denotation of a unity, an indivisible whole. It refers to the unique individuality of individuals.

The importance of understanding the patterns of behaviors can be illustrated in any typical counselor case study. No matter how much information the counselor gathers about the individual's intelligence, interests, and achievements, these data cannot speak for themselves. Until the counselor or teacher is able to see the relationship between behavior and data and observe the patter and purpose of the behavior, it is difficult to develop remedial or corrective strategies.

3. Behavior has a Purpose

According to Adler, all human behavior has a purpose. Simply stated, Adlerians think that we understand people and their behavior best in terms of their goals. If we know what a person wants, then we can best predict that person's behavior. Therefore, goal-directedness (purposiveness) is probably the most important explanation in our understanding of behavior and misbehavior.

Teleology is a term often associated with Adlerian psychology and means "purposive, moving toward goals." This teleological approach implies that the goals of behavior are always created by the individual and are not the result of preceding events, as the casual approach maintains.

Private logic is another Adlerian term that refers to the individual's cognitive constructs that serve that person's pursuit of a goal and that represent a set of "personal truths" guiding the individual. It should be mentioned that the private logic is not necessarily consistent with common sense. For example, "My mom didn't bring me a present when she returned from her business trip; therefore, she doesn't love me any more" is a statement that may make sense to a disappointed child in terms of his private logic but not in terms of what might be called "common logic."

If a teacher or counselor does not understand the private logic of the child, counseling interventions may not produce appreciable change in behavior.

Goals of children's actions. The goal-directed nature of behavior can perhaps be best understood in terms of the goals of child misbehavior. Dreikurs has written extensively about these goals and they are described in detail in Part II of this book.

4. The Striving for Significance Explains or Motivation.

Adler taught that each person strives for self-improvement, having an innate desire to become better, to become superior, or to move forward and onward. This striving for significance first takes place within the family. Sibling rivalry may be thought of as competition for unique and significant places within the family group. The striving for significance receives its direction from the individual's subjectively conceived goal of success.

Inferiority Feelings. Basic to Adlerian theory is the concept that inferiority feelings are the source of all human striving. The search for significance occurs when a person experiences the subjective feeling of being less than others and then engages in various attempts to compensate. Thus, according to Adlerian theory, feelings of inferiority are common, normal, and functional, in that they serve as motivators to movement. However, the direction taken as a result of suffering from feelings of inferiority determines whether the movement is useful or useless.

Self-Actualization. The striving for significance is in essence a movement towards the fulfillment of the goal to achieve a unique identity and to belong. Adlerians view this movement towards a unique identity as the motivating force behind all human activity. Positive attainment of the goal is generally termed "self-actualization."

Motivation and the Child's Need to Belong. Motivation can be seen in the light of the child's striving for significance — as he/she perceives significance. When interpreting children's behavior, or misbehavior, it is important that parents, teachers, or counselors recognize that a child's particular behavior, or set of behaviors, reveal how that child believes he/she fits into his/her social context at home or at school. Two useful questions that teachers and counselors might ask are, "How does this behavior help the child to be significant, as he/she perceives significance?" and "How is the child seeking to be known?"

Self-Concept. Adlerians believe that a child's way of behaving reflects his/her current concept of self. When children see themselves as inadequate in school subjects, in social interactions with peers, or unable to cope with other tasks, they tend to behave on the basis of their beliefs. For example, a child who believes he is dumb and a failure in school, may come to perceive that he can only get his teacher's attention through misbehavior.

5. Behavior is a Function of Subjective Perception

We learn to perceive life. As previously discussed, children acquire a perception of themselves and of the world around them early on in life; this is called a subjective point of view.

Phenomenology is an Adlerian term which essentially means "subjective, personal." Adlerian psychology deals with this "subjective reality" — our impressions, views, perceptions, appreceptions, or conclusions — and not with physical reality. If a child believes he/she is "dumb" or "bad," that is his/her reality.

Phenomenology has important human consequences. Consider the child who may be bright, but actually does poorly in school. This difference in ability and actual accomplishment may be due to phenomenology. The child may be discouraged, may have feelings of inferiority, may not like to study, or may want to punish his parents by doing poorly.

Psychology of use rather than possession. The above example leads to one of the maxims of Adlerian Psychology; this is a psychology of use rather than of possession. It is not what you have that counts, but rather what you do with what you have. Some children with advantages will fail while some children with disadvantages will succeed. Good grades, good behavior, and so on — the things children want to attain — are a function more of phenomenology; that is, the child's view, and not only of "facts" such as good home environment, high IQ, or favorable opportunities. Adlerians do recognize the importance of reality, of limits established by a child's heredity and environment. However, within these limits, Adlerians are more interested in what use the person makes of his/her heredity, environment, and experiences than they are of assessing these traits or qualities. By focusing on the child's motivation, decisions, and conclusions, a more practical effective teaching or counseling relationship can be achieved.

SUMMARY

Now that we have divided Adlerian psychology into many different concepts and tenets, let us see if we can assemble these assumptions into a meaningful whole. Adlerian psychology is essentially a philosophy of life, and the theory of personality that evolves is relatively simple in structure. It reaffirms the definition that people are indivisible, social, decision-making beings whose actions and psychological movement have a purpose. Each person is seen as a whole being — not an assemblage of parts — within a social setting, with a capacity to decide and choose.

THE DEVELOPMENT OF PERSONALITY

Concepts discussed in the first section of this chapter, which are pivotal in Adler's theory of personality development, included: social interest, the purposeful nature of behavior, feelings of inferiority, and striving for superiority. Other important concepts include: a realistic, not deterministic, view of biological-hereditary factors; the family constellation and family atmosphere; birth order; fictional finalism; and the life style. Many of these concepts are interrelated and overlap.

1. Heredity and Environment

In Adlerian psychology, the role of heredity in the development of personality is recognized but not emphasized. There is little, if any, empirical evidence to support genetic effects on the development of the personality. in fact, identical (one-egg) twins, who have exactly the same genetic makeup, often develop strikingly different personalities. As adults, identical twins may retell the same childhood story, but usually reach quite opposite conclusions about the incident. This supports the Adlerian position that it doesn't matter so much what we are born with or what we are born into, but what we do about it (Dinkmeyer et al, 1979).

Adlerian psychology does recognize the importance of reality, of limits set by biological-hereditary factors. A child born with deformed legs has no chance of becoming a high jumper, a child with Down's Syndrome will probably never go to college. Adlerians recognize objective reality — conditions out of and beyond the individual: physical, social, and economic factors set limits. Due to this objective reality, Adlerian psychology takes an intermediate position relative to the determinism-indeterminism point of view. They neither say "You can become anything you want" (the pure indeterministic stance) or "You are completely controlled by outside events" (the pure deterministic position) but, rather, they say, "Within the natural limits established by your biology and the environment, there is generally a lot you can do" (Manaster & Corsini, 1982).

Adlerian psychology, then, is a hopeful, positive psychology. It sees the possibility of all persons being useful and contributing members of society regardless of their native endowment or environmental circumstances.

2. The Family

The family is the primary social milieu for the young child. The various family members are the first people the baby deals with and continues to affect the child during the important developmental years. Adlerians believe that life style is fixed by the age of four to six. The family is also the primary socialization of the child. In the day-to-day interaction of the family, older family members socialize younger children, teaching them formally and informally how to behave. Adlerians would suggest that the efforts and expectations of the family should be to make the child become cooperative. Children, with what Adler would term an innate potential for social interest, want to find their place — to belong to the family. However, the child has to figure out how to belong (Manaster and Corsini, 1982).

Early in their childhood, children develop a fictional image of what they would have to be like in order to be safe, to be superior, to feel belonging, etc. (Dinkmeyer et al, 1979). This fictional image is the child's own creation, a personally developed life style based on his or her own perception of what they had to do to belong in the family. This fictional goal will be discussed later in this chapter.

3. Family Constellation

Family Constellation is a term used by Adlerians to describe the socio-psychological configuration of a family group. The personality characteristics of each family member, the emotional ties between family members, age, differences, order of birth, and dominance or submission of each member, the sex of the siblings, and the size of the family are all factors in the family constellation (Shulman & Nikelly, 1971). It is important that the counselor or school psychologist take the child's position in the family constellation into consideration in order to understand the client's personality dynamics.

4. Family Atmosphere

While the family constellation describes the interaction between members of the family, family atmosphere may be defined as the characteristic pattern established by parents and presented to their children as a standard for social living. As with family constellations, knowledge of typical family atmospheres can give the teacher, the counselor, or the school psychologist clues in understanding a child's typical pattern of behavior (lifestyle). Dewey (1971) describes a number of typical family atmospheres to which a developing child might be exposed.

The rejective atmosphere makes a child feel unaccepted, and is characterized by parents who constantly criticize and reject their children. Some parents need to learn to separate the deed from the doer; to accept the child but reject his/her misbehavior.

The authoritarian atmosphere is characterized by absolute and unquestioned obedience in the family. This type of atmosphere often produces children who are either extremely conforming or extremely rebellious.

The inconsistent atmosphere is characterized by a lack of routine and erratic and inconsistent discipline. Children in this situation don't know what is expected of them or what to expect of others.

The suppressive climate denies children the freedom to express feelings and thoughts openly and honestly . Children in this atmosphere frequently resort to daydreaming and unrealistic fantasies.

The hopeless atmosphere is characterized by discouragement and pessimism and is not uncommon in city slums and depressed rural areas. The discouragement and hopelessness that a child may feel can sometimes be overcome by an encouraging teacher or a series of successful experiences.

An overprotective or indulgent atmosphere prevents a child from learning by denying her practice in coping with difficult situations. Efforts to protect the child from unpleasantness, sadness, or failure prevents her from developing responsibility and self-reliance.

The high standards atmosphere espouses high expectations and goals. This situation can lead to children feeling the are never good enough — never meeting parental standards.

The competitive family atmosphere stresses success and each member tries to outdo the other. Competition, however, may be demonstrated in positive or negative ways. A child who cannot be "the best" in school achievement or behavior may gain some satisfaction in being "the worst" (pp. 41-45).

5. Family Values

Another dimension of the family atmosphere is family values. According to Dewey (1971), any issue which is of importance to both parents, regardless of whether they agree, becomes a family value. Each child in the family is expected to take a definite stand on the issue or value. For example, one parent may feel that school is very important; the other may think that formal education has little value. In this example, education becomes a family value. All children in this family must take a definite stand either in favor of or in opposition to school. It is not unusual to discover that maladjusted behavior in children and adolescents is often connected with the value orientation of their families.

The following quotation (Dreikurs & Cassel, 1972) serves as an excellent summary and demonstrates the tremendous influence exerted by the family atmosphere:

"If a child lives with criticism, he learns to condemn.

If a child lives with hostility, he learns to fight.

If a child lives with ridicule, he learns to be shy.

If a child lives with fear, he learns to be apprehensive.

If a child lives with shame, he learns to feel guilty.

If a child lives with tolerance, he learns to be patient

If a child lives with encouragement, he learns to be confident

If a child lives with acceptance, he learns to love.

If a child lives with recognition, he learns it is good to have a goal.

If a child lives with honesty, he learns what the truth is.

If a child lives with fairness, he learns justice.

If a child lives with security, he learns to have faith in himself and those about him.

If a child lives with friendliness, he learns the world is a nice place in which to live, to love, and be love" (pp. 28-29).

6. Birth Order

A different approach to understanding a child's behavior is through a study of the family birth order. Manaster and Corsini (1982)

maintain that Adlerian theory takes the common sense position that brothers and sisters affect each other's personality. Within any family there are parental expectations for each child based on the child's sex and birth order. Each child in a family comes to understand those expectations and his role in his own unique way. Thus, it is not uncommon to find the oldest child delegated as the parental surrogate for younger children. On the other hand, the youngest child may be pampered and spoiled by all others in the family.

PSYCHOLOGICAL BIRTH ORDER. Birth order usually refers to the sequential position of the family's children, but also of equal importance is the psychological position of the child. Adler taught that the life pattern (life style) of every child shows the imprint of her position in the family with its definite characteristics. However, no individual by virtue of birth order position always or necessarily exhibits all the traits of patterns common to persons of that birth order position. As Shulman and Mosak (1977) state: " Birth order assessment and research is often faulty because it fails to recognize that it is the psychological position of the child within the family which is crucial" (p. 118).

Manaster and Corsini (1982) would remind us that Adlerians see personality as being a complex function of one's (a) heredity, (b) social experiences, and (c) creative interpretations of heredity and social experiences. One of the determinants of personality is birth order position in the family constellation; however, it is not necessarily the major determinant.

BIRTH ORDER TERMINOLOGY. Birth order, order of birth, and ordinal position are often used synonymously and interchangeably, but in other instances they have different and exact meanings which may be contradictory. The following definitions or descriptions of selected key terms in the birth order field are recommended by Manaster (1977):

ORDINAL POSITION (ORDER OF BIRTH). "Ordinal. . . being of a specified order or rank (as second) in a numberable series." Ordinal position and order of birth should be used when indicating the numerical place of an individual's birth in the order of births in the family, as in being the first of three, or the second of four.

BIRTH ORDER. Birth order most frequently implies the following definition of order: "a category, type, class, or kind of thing of distinctive character of rank." Birth order terms (only, oldest, second, middle, and youngest) refer to categories or types of persons whose distinctive character may be known, described and, theoretically, empirically demonstrated. These birth order terms may also refer to rank in the numerical order sense, hence the source of possible confusion.

FIVE BASIC BIRTH ORDER POSITIONS. Shulman and Nikelly (1971) identify five ordinal positions (order of birth) as basic, and all other positions can be considered variations, combinations or modifications of these five. The five are identified as (1) only, (2) eldest, (3) second, (4) middle, and (5). youngest child. It is interesting to note that a child may occupy:two positions, e.g., second and youngest. A child may spend several years in one position and then find himself/herself in another, e.g., a youngest child becomes a middle child or a middle child becomes the youngest child when a younger sibling dies. Due to differences in intelligence or health, a child may be overcome or may digress into a position different from the actual order of birth, e.g., an older child by reason of physical illness may be "overrun" by a younger sibling who may function as the oldest.

General descriptions of the five basic birth order positions follow. The reader is reminded that these are generalizations and many factors influence the child's perceptions as they relate to birth order. Pepper (1971) offers the following descriptions of birth order positions and their accompanying characteristics:

Firstborn. The first child has a precarious position in life; being the oldest should entitle him/her to the favored spot, and it frequently does. However, the first child may become discouraged upon the birth of the second child. The first child .may be characterized as follows:

- An only child for a period of time, she has, therefore, been the center of interest.

- Must be first — in the sense of gaining and holding superiority over other children.

- Becomes "dethroned" with the birth of the second child. Sometimes feels unloved and neglected. May strive to keep mother's attention by positive deeds. If this fails, may adopt a pattern of uselessness or become obnoxious.

- May develop a competent behavior pattern or become discouraged.

- Sometimes strives to protect and help others in his/her struggle to keep the upper hand.

- Sometimes directs death wishes or expressions of hate toward the second child.

Second Child. The second child has an uncomfortable position in life and may try to catch up with the child in front and feel under constant pressure. The situation of the second child may be described as follows:

- Never has the undivided attention of the parents.

- Always has in front of him/her another child who is more advanced.

- Feels that the first child cannot be beaten and any claim of equality is disputed.

- May act as if in a race; hyperactivity and pushiness are often characteristics.

- If the first child is successful, the second is likely to feel uncertain of abilities.

- The second child is often the opposite of the first child. If the first child is dependable and "good;" the second may become undependable and "bad."

    - The second child becomes a "squeezed" child whenever a third child is born.

Youngest Child. The youngest child has a peculiar place in the family constellation. May become a "speeder".because he/she is outdistanced initially and may ultimately become the most successful child. On the other hand, may become discouraged and feel inferior because of the distance between himself/herself and older siblings. May exhibit some of the following traits:

    - The youngest child often behaves like an only child.

    - Decisions are often made for the youngest child and personal responsibility reduced.

    - Is often spoiled by the family.

    - Since the youngest child is usually the smallest and weakest, may not be taken seriously.

    - May become the "boss" in the family.

    - May attempt to excel in competition with siblings or may choose to evade a direct struggle for superiority.

    - May retain the baby role and place others in his/her service.

    - The youngest child often allies With the first child, since they are both seeing themselves as different from the rest.

Middle Child (of three). The middle child has an uncertain place in the family group and feels neglected. Discovers that he/she has neither the privileges of the youngest child nor the rights of the oldest. The middle child may adopt the following pattern:

    - May feel unloved and abused.

    - May hold the conviction that people are unfair to him/her.

    - May be unable to find his/her place in the group.

    - May become extremely discouraged and prone to becoming a "problem child."

However, children who come in the middle of a large family often develop stable characters and their conflict with other children tends to be less fierce. In other words, the large family generally exhibits less conflict and strife among the children.

Only Child. The only child has a decidedly difficult start in life, as he/she spends an entire childhood among persons who are bigger and more proficient. May try to develop skills in areas that will gain adult approval or may solicit adult sympathy by being shy, timid, or helpless. The only child may exhibit the following) characteristics:

- May be a pampered child.
- The only child enjoys his/her position as the center of interest.
- If the only child is a boy, he may have a mother complex. He may become convinced that he will be unable to be as strong and masculine as his father.
- May be interested only in himself/herself
- May succeed in having own way by playing mother against father.
- Sometimes the only child is taught to gain things not through his/her own effort but by depending on others.
- May feel unfairly treated when requests are not granted and may refuse to cooperate (pp. 50-53).

A concise, brief summary of the general characteristics of birth order positions is provided by Carlson (1980):

First Child. "Born first and wants to stay first." Is an only child at first and the center of interest and attention. Then feels "dethroned" by sibling. After dethronement, may seek undue attention, usually on the constructive side at first; but if he feels overrun, becomes discouraged, "a problem." Tends to:be steady responsible, dependable, conforming, and gets along well with authority figures. Frequently seen as one who has to be right, perfect and/or superior.

Second Child. "Born behind and runs hard to catch up."

Opposite of the first child: if first is "good," second is "bad" and vice versa. Chooses another field of endeavor where there is less competition from older siblings. First two children in a family usually opposites. Acts as if he were in a race: like Avis, he has to "try harder." May overcompensate, become hyperactive and "pushy."

Youngest Child. "Born the, baby, never dethroned — if it is a privilege, he never wants to leave paradise." Similar to an only child, but has siblings to observe and model from. Often "spoiled" by parents and older siblings. May not be taken seriously, since he is smallest. May lack self-reliance, act the "baby" and succeed in having things done for him. Is frequently allied with the oldest. Is frequently highly creative; may excel or evade. May become a "speeder" and become highly successful or develop feelings of inferiority and become discouraged. May remain dependent and a "baby" into adulthood.

Middle Child. "Tends to elbow self through life." Has neither the privileges of the oldest or youngest. May feel uncertain of his place, neglected and unloved. May feel people are unfair to him and that he has to struggle. Often is more sociable, but sensitive to injustice, unfairness, being slighted and feels abused. May feel squeezed.

Only Child. "A dwarf in a world of giants." Lives the formative years among persons who are bigger and more capable. Only children tend to develop a distinctive style which ensures them a place with adults; they may become very verbal, charming, intelligent or if it suits their purpose, shy and helpless."

Forer (1977) discusses some of the generalities relative to birth order which can be found in the literature. Considerable research has been conducted on this topic and the interested reader may wish to further investigate the studies cited by Forer. Brief summaries of selected studies follow:

1. First-borns frequently achieve more than do later borns especially in intellectual areas. Forer speculates that one explanation may be that mothers relate differently to their first-borns.

2. First-borns often demonstrate greater need for affiliation than

do later borns, who are frequently more independent.

3. Later borns tend to have more empathy with others than do First-borns.

4. First-borns tend to generalize more than do later borns, who tend to be more specific.

5. First-borns are likely to be more influenced' by authority and to be affected by public opinion. This responsiveness to authorities and social pressure may relate to the fact that first-borns often get more attention, positive and negative, from their parents than do later borns.

6. First-borns tend to be more fearful than are later borns. A possible explanation may be that later borns receive reassurance and are protected by the older children.

THE LIFE STYLE

Definition

In Adlerian psychology, the life style refers to a person's basic orientation toward life. It is more or less equivalent to terms such as personality, psyche, character, and ego. The. precise Adlerian term would be "style of life" — or one's unique personality. All the elements discussed so far in explaining the development of personality, add up to the dynamics of the life style (Dinkmeyer et al, 1979; Manaster & Corsini, 1982).

1. Private Logic

A person's life style is based on the individual's private logic, which was previously dIscussed in the first section of this chapter under the heading of "purposive behavior." According to Nikelly (1971), a person's whole life plan and pattern of behavior is founded on his/her private logic. This logic is consistent with and illuminates an individual's style of life in a manner similar to early recollections and the family constellation. It is within the private logic that a child forms goals, and it is these goals that explain his/her behavior rather than "needs," "drives," "conditioning," or "emotions."

2. Fictional Goal

Closely aligned with the tenet of private logic is the Adlerian concept of the fictional goal which powers the development of the life style. This concept warrants a brief explanation.

Each person develops in early childhood a fictional image of what he or she needs to do in order to be safe, to be superior, to feel belonging, or to feel complete. The attainment of this fictional image becomes the central goal of the person's life style (Dinkmeyer et al, 1979). The life plan and its fictional goal are the outcomes of the child's assessment of his or her experiences. The way in which a child perceives his experiences is affected by his internal expectations. As an individual moves through childhood she will acquire an increasing number of these perceptions.. An organized picture of his/her world emerges — partly accurate and party inaccurate. Some of these perceptions or "fictions" become concerned with future objectives or goals. This final goal may bea fiction (fictional finalism), an ideal which is impossible to realize, but which, nonetheless, is a very real spur to the individual's striving and the ultimate explanation of his or her behavior (Hall & Lindzey, 1970).

3. The Development of the Life Style
In understanding life style's development, the reader should keep in mind three basic tenets of Adlerian Psychology discussed previously: self-determination, teleology, and holism. Adlerians hold that individuals determine their own behavior, not external events. They also believe that the chosen is goal-directed and purposeful, not random. Finally, Adlerians believe that individuals cannot be subdivided into component parts, as Freud did. They view people behaving in a holistic fashion. Adlerians, then, see individuals as self-controlled people who move towards their chosen goal as unified wholes — and this is their life style (Hansen, Stevic, & Warner, 1.971).

Adler saw the development of an individual's life style taking place about the time a child reached the age of five. From that time onward the personality of the individual undergoes little change — except, of course, in the case of counseling or psychotherapy. After the first four to six years of life, each new experience usually merely confirms the person's convictions. In other words, the individual has created his/her own convictions (or fictions) about what he/she can expect of life and other people. Important to an understanding of this concept is the realization that Adler believed that the individual is not fully aware of his own life style (Hansen et al, 1977; dinkmeyer et al, 1979). Hence the importance of the counselor assisting the child and the child's parents in understanding his/her life style. This brings us to a brief discussion of life style investigation.

4. Life Style Assessment

Since the individual is holistic, Mosak,(1971) suggests that a person's lifestyle may be assessed at any point — through either past or current behavior — and through a variety of behavioral manifestations, e.g., early recollections.

Early Recollections can be considered capsule summaries of one's present life philosophy. Adler took .the view that persons remember certain incidents in their early lives to reinforce their view of themselves and their place in the world. The procedure for obtaining early recollections is simple: you ask the child to think back as far as he or she can and describe the first specific incident remembered. What the counselor wants is a recollection or specific memory as opposed to a report or general memory, such as "Every summer we used to go to my grandmother's farm." A memory has significant meaning for the individual or it wouldn't be remembered over the years. It is a statement of how life is viewed and gives clues into a person's private logic. In the opinion of Manaster and Corsini (1982), it is like an X-ray into the human mind and is a superior projective technique.

Life Style Interview. Some Adlerians prefer to do a formal analysis of a person's life style. This would involve collecting information concerning his/her family constellation, birth order, sibling relationships, parent-child relationships, family climate, and so on. However, when working with pre-adolescents, Dinkmeyer et al., (1979) suggests the use of Dreikur's four mistaken goals, which makes any formal.type of life style assessment through knowledge of the child's family constellation unnecessary.

A detailed explanation of life style assessment procedures is beyond the scope of this chapter. However, the interested reader is referred to Eckstein, Baruth, and Mahrer (1978): *Life Style: What it is and how to do it*. This excellent workbook on life style assessment and other Adlerian counseling books and materials are available from: Alfred Adler Institute, 159 North Dearborn Street, Chicago, Illinois 60601.

5. *Life Style Types*

We have already emphasized that each person has a unique life style. Keeping this fact in mind, some generalizations can be drawn about types of life styles. None of the types capsulated below are inherently bad; both constructive and non-constructive behavior can originate from life style convictions. In fact, we seldom see pure types. Most likely a person is a blend of several types. Mosak (1971) has identified fourteen possible life style types:

(1) *The baby.* The person who finds a place through the use of charm, cuteness, and the exploitation of others.

(2) *The avoider.* The person who avoids feelings may fear his own spontaneity. He lacks social presence and feels comfortable only in situations where intellectual expression is prized. His most valued techniques are logic, rationalization, intellectualization, and "Talking a good game."

(3) *The driver.* The person in motion, the "workaholic" and overachiever who nurses the fear that he is worthless.

(4) *The controller.* The person who dislikes surprises, spontaneity, and does not show his feelings because all of these "human" qualities are often uncontrollable and ungodlike.

(5) *The getter.* The person who feels he is entitled to everything in life and everyone around him. Thus, he actively or passively puts others in his service to help him get what he wants.

(6) *The opposer.* The person who actively or passively opposes everything that life demands of him.. Rather than offering positive alternative actions or ideas, he endeavors to get revenge or put down the other.

(7) *The victim.* The person who innocently or actively pursues the vocation of "disaster chaser." Everything "happens" to this individual.

(8) *The martyr.* The person who pursues the vocation of "injustice collector" and who is ready to "die for the cause," He may openly or privately endure suffering.

(9) *The inadequate one.* The person who acts as though everything he touches or does will self-destruct. Thus, he is sure to fail when given a responsibility and usually ends up putting others into his service. An underachiever.

(10) *The excitement seeker.* The person who despises routine and seeks out the novel experiences in life. He endeavors to stimulate excitement when life appears dull. Alone or in league with others, he will engage in spontaneous and often senseless behaviors.

(11) *The right one.* The person who elevates himself above others whom he arranges to perceive as being wrong. He avoids error like the plague, and will rationalize his way out of an actual error, convincing you that you are more wrong than he is.

(12) *The good one.* The person who constantly lives by higher moral standards than others. He cannot forgive or forget and constantly blames and reminds you of your shortcomings.

(13) *The pleaser.* The person who needs to be liked feels required to please everyone all the time and is particularly sensitive to critics. Sees the evaluations of others as the yardstick of his worth.

(14) *The superior one.* The person who needs to be superior may refuse to enter life tasks in which he will not be seen as the "center" or the "best." If he cannot attain superiority through being first or best, he often settles for being last worst (pp. 78-80).

ADLERIAN PSYCHOLOGY AND EDUCATIONAL APPLICATIONS

1. The Contemporary Classroom

Principles of Adlerian psychology can be quite useful in educational settings. Dinkmeyer and Dinkmeyer (1983) identify the following situations as common in contemporary classrooms:

(a) Teachers frequently report that discipline is their main problem — almost regardless of grade level — and that traditional disciplinary approaches, which rely on unquestioning respect of authority, often don't seem to work.

(b) Classroom teachers, and many counselors, are frequently untrained or poorly prepared to work with groups, the most basic teaching skill.

(c) Many teachers appear to be attempting to function in the classroom without a practical understanding of human behavior.

(d) In many classrooms the affective domain is ignored in the rush to "return to the basics." Developing an understanding of self and others should be a central goal in the educational process (p. 311).

Dinkmeyer and Dinkmeyer (1983) further suggest that Adlerian psychology can be appropriately applied to the educational process in three major areas:

(1) Building awareness of self and enhancing feelings of self-worth. It is universally accepted that academic achievement is highly correlated with positive feelings and self-worth. Our curriculum must include an affective component to assist the child in developing an understanding of self and others.

(2) Taking advantage of positive group forces. Every classroom has its own unique classroom dynamics. Through the/use of Adlerian principles, the teacher may become aware of these interrelationships among the children and between the teacher and the children. The classroom meeting is offered as an example of a technique which recognizes the value of a group and gives a democratic outlet for problem solving.

(3) Handling discipline in a logical and non-punitive manner. Discipline which provides for a mutual sharing of power is more efficient and much less wearing on both teachers and students. Each child is given the opportunity to learn from his or her choice, within a mutually agreed upon classroom "code of conduct." This approach, logical consequences, is part of the Adlerian approach to classroom discipline and is discussed in detail in Part III.

According to Brooks (1971), Adler firmly believed that maladjustments in later life could be significantly reduced if educational measures were systematically applied by teachers early in the child's life so that he/she would be better prepared to meet the tasks of adulthood. He believed that the school — not society in general — is the child's best teacher, provided that it developed his potential for social interest and helped him/her to exercise freedom with equal attention paid to developing responsibility. This is also the stance taken by Glasser (1969, 1972) in many of his writings. Brooks (1971) says that two basic concepts need to be established when cultivating responsibility and self-discipline: (1) that the idea of interrelationship applies to the classroom, i.e., "what kind of class would we have if every student was just like me?"; and (2) cultivating self-worth or self-value. Brooks (1971), in developing a climate for personality growth and in building social feeling, has recommended the following principles:

(1) Make each child feel that she is important to the group, that her help with work is needed, that her ideas are worth considering in connection with class problems, and that her participation in class activities is vital to all.

(2) Praise effort involved rather than actual achievement. Get beneath surface talents and respond to the slow, discouraged child as well as to the quick, show-off or talented youngster.

(3) Avoid all mention of "good," "bad," "better," "best" in characterizing children or their behavior.

(4) Never fight verbally (or physically, of course) with a child.

Maintain an attitude of good will — an expectation that the child wants to do her part. In the case of a child who refuses, recognize that we cannot meet the difficulty with force but must work it out matter-of-factly through natural consequences or through mutual agreement after discussion.

(5) Never humiliate a child in private or in a group (p. 194).

2. Counseling Techniques

It is generally accepted that counseling children younger than five or six years of age requires the active involvement of the parents. According to Dinkmeyer and Dinkmeyer (1983), this counseling is actually a form of family counseling. Corsini (1971) notes that it was Alfred Adler, who, in about 1921, began interviewing and counseling parents in front of other parents and professionals. This method of demonstration served to change the observers as well as the counselees. This method of open family counseling, is the oldest form of group psychotherapy in use today.

By the age of five or six, Adlerians believe that children's language and cognitive abilities have usually progressed to a point that they are ready for individual or group counseling, as well as family counseling. Among the Adlerian techniques and principles appropriate for children are those discussed by Dinkmeyer and Dinkmeyer (1983):

(1) Don't talk down to children. It is confusing for a child to hear an adult attempt to talk like a child. Counselors should use their own words and tone of voice, taking into consideration the restrictive vocabulary of the child.

(2) Many nonverbal modes, such as music, art, or puppetry can be fruitful avenues of communication with young children, as well as an adjunct to the counseling process.

(3) Play therapy is probably more useful as a diagnostic tool than a mode of counseling.

(4) Counselors need to recognize the importance of working with the child's entire world. The child's world includes parents,

grandparents, siblings, teachers, and significant others. Changes in the adults around the child often generate change in the child.

(5) To effectively influence a child's attitudes and behavior, the counselor needs to understand the child's perceptions. Adlerian child counseling often includes a life style assessment.

(6) Children will respond to and learn much from confrontation and tentative interpretation. An example of tentative interpretation can be found in the "Could it be . . . ?" questions used in connection with the four goals of behavior (See Part II of this book).

(7) When counseling children, it is important to go beyond insight into the action phase of counseling. In other words, assist the child in developing a plan to put the concepts she has learned into action.

(8) Effective child counseling involves contact with the significant others in the child's life. When both parents and teachers are involved, a greater impact is made upon the behavior of the child (pp. 302-303, 306).

Summary

Counselors often consult with teachers and parents about children's discipline problems. Adlerian counselors are not content to deal with the observed behavior alone; they will try to understand the purpose of the the child's behavior. Only if the adult — be it teacher or parent — understands the child's mistaken behavior are they able to cooperatively plan helpful approaches with the child (Dinkmeyer et al., 1979).

It is important for the counselor to try to bring about a general agreement among the parents, the school personnel, and the child concerning the best course of action. Frequently, the school blames the parents and the parents blame the school, while the child avoids responsibility for his behavior. According to Dinkmeyer et al. (1979), counselors must recognize that most teachers are well qualified to teach children who want to learn but often don't know effective alternatives for dealing with children who don't want to learn or don't want to behave. Therefore, the counselor must be knowledgeable and willing to serve as both teacher and consultant to teachers and parents concerning the basic principles of child rearing and human development. The author hopes that this book will serve as a resource for counselors and teachers in fulfilling this consultant role.

REFERENCES

Adler, A. (1927). *Understanding human behavior*. New York; Garden City Publishers.

Brooks, M. H. (1971). The cultivation of responsibility and self-discipline. In A. G. Nikelly (Ed.), *Techniques for, behavior change* (pp. 191-196). Springfield, IL: Charles C. Thomas.

Carlson, J. (1980). *Life style handout*. Paper presented at the 1980 APGA Convention Program on Adlerian Counseling, Atlanta, GA.

Corsini, R. J. (1971). Group psychotherapy. In A. G. Nikelly (Ed.), *Techniques for behavior change* (pp. 111-115). Springfield, IL: Charles C. Thomas.

Dewey, E. A. (1971). Family Atmosphere. In A. G. Nikelly (Ed.), *Techniques for behavior change* (pp. 41-47). Springfield, IL: Charles C. Thomas.

Dinkmeyer, D. C., & Dinkmeyer, D. C., Jr. (1983). Adlerian approaches. In H. T. Prout & D. T. Brown (Eds.) *Counseling and psychotherapy with children and adolescents: Theory and practice for school and clinic settings* (pp. 289-327). Tampa, FL: Mariner.

Dinkmeyer, D. C., Pew, W. L., & Dinkmeyer, D. C., Jr. (1979). *Adlerian counseling and psychotherapy*. Monterey, CA: Brooks/Cole.

Dreikurs, R. & Cassel, P. (1972). *Discipline without tears* (2nd ed.). New York: Hawthorne Books.

Eckstein, D., Baruth, L., &Mahrer, D. (1978). *Life style: What it is and how to do it*. Dubuque, IA: Kendall/Hunt.

Forer, L. K. (1977). The use of birth order information in psychotherapy. *Journal of Individual Psychology, 33,* 105-113.

Glasser, W. (1969). *Schools without failure*. New York: Harper & Row.

Glasser, W. (1972). *The identity society*. New York: Harper & Row.

Hall, C. S. & Lindzey, G. (1970). *Theories of personality* (2nd ed.). New York: J. Wiley & Sons.

Hansen, J. C., Stevic, R. R., & Warner, R. W., Jr.(1977). *Counseling: Theory and process* (2nd ed.). Boston: Allyn and Bacon.

Hansen, J. C., Warner, R. W., & Smith, E. J. (1980). *Group counseling: Theory and process* (2nd ed.). Chicago: Rand McNally

Manaster, G. J. (1977). *Birth order: An-overview. Journal of Individual Psychology, 33,* 3-8.

Manaster, G. J., & Corsini, R. J. (1982). *Individual psychology: Theory and practice.* Itasca, IL: Peacock.

Mosak, H. H. (1971). Lifestyle. In A. G. Nikelly (Ed.), *Techniques for behavior change* (pp. 77-81). Springfield; IL: Charles C. Thomas.

Mosak, H. H. (1984). Adlerian psychotherapy. In R.J. Corsini (Ed.), *Current psychotherapies* (3rd ed.), (pp. 56-107). Itasca, IL: Peacock.

Nikelly, A. G. (1971). Private logic. In A. G. Nikelly (Ed.); *Techniques for behavior change* (pp. 61-64). Springfield, IL: Charles C. Thomas.

Pepper, F. C. (1971). Birth order. In A. G. Nikelly (Ed.), *Techniques for behavior change* (pp. 49-54). Springfield, IL: Charles C. Thorilas.

Shulman, B. H. & Mosak, H. H. (1977). Birth order and ordinal position: Two Adlerian views. *Journal of Individual Psychology, 33,*114-121.

Shulman, B. H., & Nikelly, A. G. (1971). Family constellation. In A. G. Nikelly (Ed.), *Techniques for behavior change* (pp. 35-40). Springfield, IL: Charles C. Thomas.

PART I

---

*An Overview of
Adlerian Psychology*

THE FOUR GOALS OF MISBEHAVIOR

Definition

Dreikurs (1968) classified all child misbehavior into four cate-gories, each corresponding to the goal of the misbehavior: attention, power, revenge, and display of inadequacy.

Every action of a child ,has a purpose. The child's basic pur-pose or aim is to achieve his/her place in a group. The four goals of disturbing behavior can be observed in all young children up to the age of ten. However, any child's goal may vary occasionally depending on the circumstances; he/she may "act up" to attract attention at one moment, and seek revenge at another.

Dreikurs has been accused of arbitrarily putting every disturb-ing behavior of a child in one of these four categories. Dreikurs did not invent these categories, but systematically and consistently observed them. In his own defense, Dreikurs (1968) invites his critics to show other goals of misbehaving young children which could be incorporat-ed into his model. The four goals can also be observed in adolescents and adults, but according to Dreikurs, they are not all-inclusive. There may be other ways that pre-teens and teenagers can find their place in a destructive way, through sexual experimentation, smoking, drug and alcohol abuse, gang membership, and other means of excitement.

Each goal is examined in detail, as explained by Dreikurs (1968), Dinkmeyer, Pew, and Dinkmeyer (1979), and Lowe (1971).

1. Attention

The attention-getting mechanism (AGM) is operative in most young children. "Am I a part of the family group? Are you noticing me? Do I have status and recognition in the class?" may express the purpose of the child's attention-seeking behavior.

A child may first try to gain attention through socially accept-able and pleasant means. However, when these efforts are no longer effective, the child will try any other conceivable method to put others into his service or to get attention. Humiliation, punishment, or even physical pain in the form of spanking do not matter as long as the child achieves his/her purpose. He/she prefers those attentions to being ignored; then the child is sure that he/she is lost and has no place in the family or group.

2. Power

Efforts to control the child lead to a deadlock in a struggle for power and superiority between a child and adults. The child attempts to prove that he can do what he wants and can refuse to do what the adult requires or demands.

The power-seeking child is often guided by the faulty belief "I can obtain a place in this world only if I am in control of significant others." Any adult — parent or teacher — who lets himself be drawn into a struggle for power with a child is lost. No final "victory" of parents or teachers is possible.. In most instances, the child will "win out," if only because he/she is not restricted in his fighting methods by any strong sense of responsibility or moral obligation. If the parent or teacher chooses to struggle with the child to determine who, in fact, is more powerful, a battle may be won while the war is lost. Once a power conflict ensues, the relationship between the child and adult can only further deteriorate and the child may move to the next goal, revenge.

3. Revenge

A battle between parents or teachers and the child for power and domination may reach a point where the adult will try every conceivable means to control the child. However, the mutual antagonism may become so strong that each party has only one desire: retaliation to revenge their feeling of being hurt.

Children are often aware of certain misbehaviors that are particularly irritating to parents or teachers, and may choose to utilize them in their goal of revenge. The parent or teacher, unaware of the goal of the child's behavior, is likely to be utterly confused, by what appears to be the child's senseless need to hurt and will often return the revenge in kind, thus perpetuating the cycle. Children caught up in this cycle know where they can hurt the most and take advantage of the vulnerability of their adversaries. If they regard it as a triumph that can be obtained, it may be the only one they seek.

4. Display of Inadequacy

The intense fight between adult and child can lead to an extreme form of discouragement, either to the full negative of social participation, as in the revengeful child, or to the full denial of any capacity. The child may expect only defeat or failure and stop trying. He hides himself behind a display of real or imagined inferiority. The child uses this inadequacy as protection so that nothing will be required or expected of her. By avoiding participation or contribution, she thinks she can avoid more .humiliating and embarrassing situations.

FOUR TYPES OF BEHAVIOR

In pursuing one or more of these goals, children may be either active or passive and may — as in the case of attention getting — use constructive or destructive methods. According to Dreikurs (1968), if the child feels accepted he will use constructive methods, whereas antagonism is always expressed in destructive acts. On the other hand, the basic pattern of activity or passivity is established in early childhood and depends on the child's self- confidence. This pattern is often difficult to change.

These two pairs of factors lead to four types of behavior:

1. Active-constructive
2. Active-destructive
3. Passive-constructive
4. Passive-destructive

Dreikurs (1968) and Lowe (1971) give examples of these four basic patterns using characteristic behavior patterns often found in school children. Active-constructive behavior is usually based on the child's desire to be first in the class, to be on task, and to be recognized for being good — maybe the "teacher's pet."

Active-destructive behavior is usually exhibited through some form of "acting up." The child may seek attention by being a bully, acting defiant, playing around as the class clown, or showing off in class.

Passive-constructive behavior is exhibited when the child receives a favorable position through inactivity. The child gains approval by being particularly charming and by always doing what she is told. This behavior is usually appreciated by adults who may respond with comments to other children like "I wish you could be as quiet as Nancy" or "Marcus never gives me any trouble."

With passive-destructive behavior the child tends to withdraw, in the hopes that the adult will prod or offer encouragement. The child may use such techniques as laziness, stubbornness, excessive eating, stammering, being shy, bashful, or late, and other displays of inadequacy. The child may respond favorably to persistent correction, but that response is short lived. The adult may not immediately realize that considerable time (and attention) has been expended trying to get the child to do whatever the adult has been trying to get her to do.

At this point, it is important to remind the reader-that the behavior per se gives us little or no indication as to the child's goal or purpose for engaging in that behavior. It is in the process of verification (goal recognition) that this determination is made.

GOAL RECOGNITION

According to Dreikurs, Grunwald, and Pepper (1971), no child is fully aware of why he behaves as he does. Only a very few of the child's intentions reach the conscious level. Often when a child is asked why he did something wrong, he simply doesn't know. Parents and teachers sometimes become frustrated and angry when the child openly responds to their question of why he did it, with "I don't know," which is actually the truth. Since the child is not aware of his own motive, if the child gives an explanation it is usually a rationalization.

Even though conscious purposiveness relatively rare in young children's misbehavior, Bitter (1991) has suggested three additional goals which could be added to Dreikurs' typology. These conscious goals are getting, self evaluation, and avoidance. Should the Dreikursian goals be ruled out, these conscious goals may add another frame of.reference for the counselor or clinician.

Recognition Reflex

The trained counselor or teacher (or parent) can help the child:become aware. When the goal of her disturbance is disclosed to her, the child usually responds with a recognition reflex. Dreikurs, et. al.(1971), defines this recognition reflex as a peculiar smile or glint in the eyes indicating the child has suddenly become aware of her goal and is beginning to understand why she is acting in a certain way. More importantly, she realizes that the adult also understands the goal behind her behavior. It is important for diagnostic purposes to solicit the recognition reflex; such confrontation with her goals can be the first step towards a plan for a change in behavior. Nothing is accomplished when the parent or teacher tells the child what she is — lazy, aggressive, untruthful, or other disturbing behavior. Even if that were accurate, it does not mean anything to the young child. It is different, however, when she is confronted with her goals — the intentions behind her behavior(s). Then alternatives appear because the child can decide whether she wants to continue or not.

THE "COULD IT BE...?" QUESTION

Dinkmeyer (1971) and Lowe (1971) has suggested a mild form of confrontation to solicit the recognition reflex. They suggest the "Could it be...?" question. Utilizing this technique, the counselor or teacher suggests the goal or intention behind the child's behavior in a non-threatening confrontation. If delivered in a caring, concerned manner, the "Could it be...?" question does not come through as an indictment or accusation against the child,

Applying the "Could it be...?" Question Technique:

The chart on the following page illustrates how to use the "Could it be...?" question technique to identify the goals of children's misbehavior. Dreikurs and Cassel (1972) indicate that all four questions should be asked of the child in the order listed even though the goal may be already suspected. This chart was adapted from a more detailed presentation by Dreikurs and Cassel (1972) and Dinkmeyer (1971).

According to Dreikurs and Cassel (1972), in preparation for the "Could it be. . ." confrontation technique, the conversation between the child and adult may go something like this:

ADULT: (Teacher or Parent): "Do you know why you did _____?" (whatever the misbehavior was.)

CHILD: "No." (At a conscious level the child probably doesn't know.)

ADULT: "Would you like to know? I have some ideas if you are willing to listen."

CHILD: "Yes." (The child will usually be interested.)

ADULT: (In a non judgmental, friendly manner ask all four of the "Could it be . . .?" questions. All four questions are asked sequentially because the child may be operating on more than one goal at a time.)

IDENTIFYING THE GOALS OF CHILDREN'S MISBEHAVIOR USING THE "COULD IT BE...?" QUESTION TECHNIQUE

CHILD'S ACTION		PROBABLE GOAL	"COULD IT BE...?" QUESTION
Active Destructive	**Passive Destructive**	**What the Teacher or Parent suspects is the goal**	Questions must be asked non-judgmentally
"Nuisance" show-off or clown restless minor mischief acts "tough"	**"Laziness"** bashfulness lack of ability fearfulness poor performance	**Goal 1: Attention getting** Child seeks proof of his approval or status (common w/ preschoolers). Puts others in his service, seeks help. Will cease when given attention (positive or negative).	**ATTENTION** A "Could it be that you want me to notice you?" OR B "Could it be that you want me to do something special for you?"
"Rebel" argues and contradicts defies authority ... untruthfulness refuses to do work	**"Stubborn"** extreme laziness disobedience forgetting stubbornness	**Goal 2: Power** Similar to attention getting, but more intense. Reprimand intensifies misbehavior. Wants to be the boss.	**POWER** A "Could it be that you want to show me that you can do what you want and no one can stop you?" OR B "Could it be that you want to be boss?"
"Vicious" stealing violent, and sometimes brutal bed-wetting	**"Violent Passivity"** sullen defiant	**Goal 3: Revenge** Tries to hurt others (as he feels hurt by them). Makes self hated. Retaliates, gets even.	**REVENGE** A "Could it be that you want to hurt me and/or the children in the class?" OR B "Could it be that you want to get even?"
	"Hopelessness" stupidity indolence inaptitude inferiority complex	**Goal 4: Display of Inadequacy** Assumes real or imagined deficiency. Wants to be left alone, feels helpless. Doesn't want anyone to know how stupid he thinks he is.	**DISPLAY OF INADEQUACY** A "Could it be that you want to be left alone?" OR B "Could it be that you feel stupid and don't want people to know?"

How to Solve Behavior Problems
Using the Adlerian/Dreikursian Approach

The reader is reminded by Dreikurs (1972) that the unconscious goal is often the unadmitted goal. When diagnosing the child's misbehavior, using the "Could it be...?" technique, it is advisable to consider the following points:

1. What does the behavior really say about the child's purpose?
2. What was the adult's (teacher or parent) feeling in response to the misbehavior?
3. What did the adult possibly do to reinforce the child's misbehavior (mistaken goal)?
4. What could be the child's next move if corrective procedures are not implemented?

Some examples of typical behavior problems of elementary school children are given to illustrate each of the four goals of misbehavior:

EXAMPLE 1: ATTENTION

CHILD'S BEHAVIOR:
Peggy has interrupted class instruction without raising her hand for permission (a class rule) the fifth time this morning. This behavior has persisted for the past several weeks.

ADULT'S REACTION:
The teacher feels annoyed. She has reminded Peggy to ask for permission to talk by raising her hand and has reprimanded her for her behavior. The teacher feels that Peggy is requiring too much of her teaching time.

CORRECTIVE PROCEDURE(S):

As in each of the other examples to follow, after the teacher has confirmed her suspicion by the "Could it be...?" confrontation technique, and by seeing the recognition reflex, she can apply corrective procedures. The teacher will ignore Peggy when she speaks out of turn and interrupts, but will talk to her later. The teacher will comment on Peggy's cooperative behavior whenever possible and show an interest in her, but never at a time when Peggy demands or expects it. Hopefully, Peggy will come to realize that she is accepted by the teacher and does belong to the class group.

EXAMPLE 2: POWER

CHILD'S BEHAVIOR:

Robert has just thrown a paper wad across the classroom. The teacher has asked him to write a social studies assignment, but he is openly disobedient and continues to throw spitballs. He is in a particularly defiant mood today, has argued with classmates, and has not completed a single assignment.

ADULT'S REACTION:

The teacher feels defeated and that her leadership of the class is threatened. The teacher thinks "Who is running this class? He or I?" She yells, "Robert, this behavior cannot continue another minute!"

CORRECTIVE PROCEDURE(S):

As discussed previously, a power struggle with a child who has this goal is a no win situation. The teacher needs to withdraw from conflict, which will usually take the wind out of the child's sails. The teacher will recognize and may openly admit defeat. She will recognize Robert's power and try to get him to use it constructively by enlisting his cooperation and giving him some classroom or group responsibility. The teacher will remain kind and firm, but will avoid an open power struggle. In a time of less turmoil, better alternatives can be explored.

EXAMPLE 3: REVENGE

CHILD'S BEHAVIOR:

Rob refuses to complete his math assignment and simply scribbles on his paper. He also marks in his math textbook. Rob is sullenly defiant. When he plays ball with the other boys he sometimes becomes violent and kicks or hits his schoolmates. On one occasion, after the principal had punished him, he returned to the classroom and pushed over the class aquarium.

ADULT'S REACTION:

The teacher feels hurt and outraged by Rob's behavior. She wishes Rob were not in her class. The teacher wonders how Rob can be so mean, especially to the other children. Often an initial reaction may be to get even.

CORRECTIVE PROCEDURE(S):

Even though the teacher feels like "getting even" and letting Rob know how hurt she is, she avoids such acknowledgement. She decides not to shout at him again and avoids punishment. Instead, she tries to win the child by doing unexpected things that surprise and please him. She encourages the group to like and support him. She may ask for a volunteer to be his "buddy" and assist him with class assignments.

EXAMPLE 4: DISPLAY OF INADEQUACY

CHILD'S BEHAVIOR:

Dyanna has withdrawn and never participated in class discussions or activities. Most of the time she can be observed starring blankly at. the wall or out of the window. She seems to be saying subconsciously, "Leave me alone. I can't do anything right so I'm not going to try. I'm no good; stupid.

Adult's Reaction:
The teacher feels helpless and doesn't know what to do. After attempts at correction fail, the teacher may believe that the child is truly unable to perform. However, this is usually pseudo stupidity and/or an inferiority complex be it real or imagined.

CORRECTIVE PROCEDURE(S):
The teacher will resist "giving up." She will attempt to make Dyanna feel worthwhile when she tries and offer her encouragement, particularly when she makes mistakes. Even young children are influenced by their peer group; therefore, the teacher will enlist the help of the class. Peer helpers may be a viable approach. The basic ideas is to show Dyanna that others have faith in her abilities to cope, and to offer encouragement with each approximation.

ADDITIONAL RESOURCES

Dreikurs and Cassel (1972) and Dinkmeyer, et. al. (1979) offer additional examples of dealing with the four goals of misbehavior in the classroom setting. Dinkmeyer and McKay (1997) have developed a program for training parents in effectively managing behavior program entitled "Systematic Training for Effective Parenting" is widely utilized by school counselors, school psychologists, and others to help train parents to cope with their children's behavior. This program and its spin-offs "Step/Teen" and "Early Childhood Step" will prove to be a valuable resource for the person interested in the Adlerian/ Dreikursian approach to discipline.

References

Bitter, J.R. (1991). Conscious motivations: An enhancement to Dreikur's goals of children's misbehavior. *Individual Psychology, 47* (2). 210-221.

Dinkmeyer, D. C., Sr., & McKay, G. D. (1997). *STEP: Systematic training for effective parenting* (4th ed.). Circle Pines, MH: American Guidance Service.

Dinkmeyer, D. C. (1971). The "C" group: Integrating knowledge and experience to change behavior — an Adlerian approach to consultation. *The Counseling Psychologist, 3,* (1) 63-72.

Dinkmeyer, D. C., Pew, W. L., & Dinkmeyer, D. C., Jr. (1979). Adlerian counseling and psychotherapy. Monterey, CA; Brooks/Cole.

Dreikurs, R,(1968). *Psychology in the classroom* (2nd ed.). New York; Harper & Row.

Dreikurs, R., & Cassel, P. (1972). *Discipline without tears* (2nd ed.). New York; Hawthorn.

Dreikurs, R., Grunwald, B. B., & Pepper, F. C. (1971). *Maintaining sanity in the classroom: Illustrated teaching techniques.* New York; Harper & Row.

Lowe, R. N. (19n). Goal recognition. In A.G. Nikelly (Ed.). *Techniques for behavior change* (pp. 65-75). Springfield, lL; Charles C. Thomas.

PART III

Natural and Logical
Consequences:
Adlerian Disciplinary Techniques

INTRODUCTION

"The problems that our children present are increasing in frequency and intensity, and many parents do not know how to cope with them" (Dreikurs., 1964). Although written over twenty-five years ago, these opinions held or debated by parents and teachers alike. The solutions proposed each decade have varied, but the approaches that are based on the Individual Psychology of Alfred Adler promote discipline as the development of personal responsibility, and suggest that parents be neither punitive nor permissive. Instead, parents who come to a better understanding of the reasons that children misbehave will be making the first step towards effective parenting. Learning the skills of encouragement, consistency, and the use of natural and logical consequences can assist parents in their most important work; guiding a child's behavioral development so that "he can respond correctly to the demands of social life" (Adler, 1963, p.3).

Democratic Discipline Principles

Dinkmeyer and Dreikurs (1963) suggest that the "traditional methods of influencing children come from an autocratic past when reward and punishment were the effective means of influencing and stimulating subordinates and promoting conformity to the demands of authorities like parents and teachers" (p.2). To accomplish the transition from autocratic to democratic methods of child guidance, parents and educators must encourage choices and responsibility. Democratic relationships are central to effective behavior training and a respect for order. To maintain order is encouragement, and a respect for order. To maintain order is essential, and to do so depends upon clear expectations and experiencing natural consequences for misbehavior.

REWARDS AND PUNISHMENT

Although our country champions democratic ideals, many educators and parents have not made the transition into treating their children with democratic principles. Instead, they have continued to attempt to control and dominate children with rewards and punishment. These external pressures generally yield short-term results that must be continually repeated to be effective (Dinkmeyer & McKay, 1983).

1. Rewards

Rewards usually are given by someone in a superior role to someone in an inferior position, which is not a mutually respectful stance. They are often used as "bribes" which in the end teaches that nothing worthwhile is given freely. Rewards given by parents often come back to haunt them when children refuse to do anything unless they receive a tangible reward. The focus is removed from internal controls to external ones (Dreikurs, 1971).

To illustrate, look at Sam, who at age seven was given a small toy by his mother each time he behaved in the grocery store. When he began to pester for similar rewards in other situations, mom became exasperated. Was she teaching him to modify his behavior or learn to bargain? If children are taught that everything worth doing must be compensated, when are they to learn and feel the value of giving and helping?

2. Punishment

Curwin and Mendler (1988) point out that punishment is a form of retribution; often more of a release of the punisher's frustration. Venting anger and making children "pay" for their misbehavior is a short-sighted, selfish way to handle problem situations. When punished, children learn to go underground with their behavior, if not choosing to directly challenge the authority figure.

Gordon (1981) presents very convincing arguments against rewards and punishment, including data which suggest that harsh punishment may promote aggressive behavior in children. Punishment teaches that power and control. are the ultimate weapons. Young people who are frequently punished harbor resentment, anger, and often feel that they have the right to punish their parents. When punishment becomes physical, it's as if permission has been granted to become physically aggressive and many times even abusive. Gordon cites Hyman (1975) whose study showed that schools using physical punishment had more vandalism than schools that did not. Also cited was Martin's (1975) study of juvenile delinquents, which found a pattern of power-assertive punishment among parents and those delinquents.

PUNISHMENT VERSUS LOGICAL CONSEQUENCES

Further clarifying the differences between punishment and logical consequences, Dinkmeyer compares the two as opposites (Shiff, 1987):

PUNISHMENT	LOGICAL CONSEQUENCES
emphasis on power, demands personal authority	recognizes mutual respect and rights
arbitrary, no logic	direct relationship to behavior
moral judgments	no moral judgments; separates deed and doer
concerned with past behavior	present and future are important
treats child with disrespect	invoked in friendly, calm manner
demands obedience	permits choice

Not only are the messages sent to children vastly different when punishment is used instead of logical consequences, but the resulting actions and thoughts of the children are quite opposite as well. The following chart is adapted from Dinkmeyer's writings on this subject:

PUNISHMENT

Characteristic:	Child is likely to be:
emphasis on power, authority	rebellious, sneaky, irresponsible, vengeful
arbitrary	resentful, afraid, confused, vengeful, and rebellious
morally judgmental	guilty, hurt
emphasis on past behavior	unsure of self-worth, insecure in decision-making
threats of loss of love or violence	afraid, rebellious, guilty, vengeful
demanding of compliance	rebellious, defiant in compliance

LOGICAL CONSEQUENCES

Characteristic:	Child is likely to be:
mutually respectful cooperative, reliable, self-disciplined	respectful of self and others
logically related to event	learning from experience
separates deed and doer	secure in self-worth
concern with present and future	self-directing and self-evaluating

Remember that the overriding goal, in using natural and logical consequences is to motivate children to make responsible choices, not to force them into submission. Patience and consistency must prevail.

Building Responsibility

According to Adlerians, good discipline "builds within the child the courage to function effectively" (Dinkmeyer, 1965, p. 303). Confidence is also built when a child experiences her own strengths and abilities, comes to see her responsibility to her family and social group, and moves towards the internalization of control. The use of natural and logical consequences is a technique which offers opportunities for children to discover these capabilities.

Eight year old Maria loves to help her mother in the kitchen, and when she decided to bake cookies by herself without permission, she burned them, making a big mess in the process. How can this situation be handled in a way which promotes Maria's sense of responsibility?

First her; mother could acknowledge the feelings involved, "Oh Maria, you must have been very frightened when all your hard work burned in the oven!" Then after the tears were dried, Mother would need to structure the consequences, not punishment, giving Maria the tools to correct her problem. She might tell her how to clean the encrusted cookie sheet, then allow Maria to do the work herself. Later, the two might sit down and discuss reasonable rules for cooking when Mother is not present. How easy it would have been for Mother to yell at Maria, banning her from the kitchen and making Maria feel very incompetent indeed. Instead, the logical consequences preserve Maria's dignity and help her learn from the experience.

NATURAL AND LOGICAL CONSEQUENCES

Explanation of Terms

Although the term "consequences" may encompass both natural and logical consequences, a distinction can be made. Natural consequences represent reality with no interference from adults. Getting cold when going out to play without a coat is a natural consequence which allows the child to learn from the experience. Denying a child the privilege of watching a TV program because of not wearing a coat is punishment which will not foster responsibility, but may encourage rebellion and resentment (Dinkmeyer, 1989).

Dinkmeyer, Dinkmeyer, and McKay (1987) advocate letting a child go hungry if he misses breakfast, for example. Their point is that the child controls when he eats, not the parent. Most parents would become very upset if the child continued to leave home without eating. Then it seems appropriate to find out why the child isn't eating. Is this the child who dislikes traditional breakfast food? If so, preparing alternatives or allowing the child to select his own breakfast might be a solution. Or, if allowed at school, perhaps a snack for later might be helpful to the child who is unable to eat soon after rising.

Logical consequences are those which follow a violation of the social order, or what it takes to live cooperatively within society. They can be as simple as allowing a child to take the consequences at school of forgetting to take lunch money, or as structured as helping a child choose how to handle losing a friend's toy. Whenever possible, choices offered with respect, not threats, work best. Children can be encouraged to help list the choices, learning to take responsibility for their own problems and solutions instead of always relying on adults around them to come up with solutions, as the following example illustrates (Dinkmeyer, 1989).

A student expressed concern over all the coats and hats on the classroom floor. Another child suggested that anything found on the floor either be thrown away or put into the "lost and found." The whole class voted to put items into the "lost and found." The teacher merely monitored this progress. When items were scattered as usual, two children loaded them all into the "lost and found" box. Then when recess bell sounded, quite a few children lost time rummaging through the box looking for their coats and hats. Each day the number of clothes on the floor decreased. Within a week, the problem had been solved by the children, not the teacher (Dreikurs and Cassel, p. 90, 91).

Dreikurs (1964) insists that the responsibilities and consequences of actions belong to children and are not the domain of the parents. The role parents and teachers have is to carefully select words which let children know that they have the power to choose and act. When children experience this power, their independence and confidence is strengthened. However, many adults simply wish to dominate children and when control is the issue, children rarely learn the power of their own choices. If the "logical" consequence is contrived, and not really related to the misbehavior, then the adult's goals are suspect. Power and control have become the issue rather than the correction of a problem situation.

As Dreikurs (1971) reminds us, a child must come to understand why he behaves as he does, how this behavior affects others, how it is "successful" behavior from the child's point of view, and how appropriate behavior can gain him more acceptance. Unless we accomplish these goals, the use of natural and logical consequences becomes merely a temporary tool. The selection of a logical consequence also depends a great deal upon the goal of the child as well as his method of obtaining it. Karen, who rarely disturbs the class, may benefit from being isolated for a few minutes. However, the same consequence may not be appropriate for Michael, who disturbs class frequently.

With Michael, you could begin with a private conversation about his constant talking. "Could it be that you want my attention much of the time?" You could then ask Mike how many times he thought he needed that attention during a class period. Since most children won't give a number, you could suggest fifteen times. Even if Mike protests that fifteen is too many times, stick with it. Then each time Michael talks out, say "Michael, that's one; Michael, that's two." Usually fifteen is never reached because this kind of attention is not fun, nor does it get a response from classmates. If you slip and say, "Michael I've told you about this talking; I'm giving you one more chance before I start counting," then the technique has been subverted. You need to remember to be consistent, brief, and unemotional.

Employing Consequences

In his book, *The Effective Parent*, Dinkmeyer and his associates (1987) summarize guidelines for using consequences effectively:

• identify the goal of the behavior
• recognize who owns the problem
• give logical choices and follow through
• negotiate consequences if appropriate
• choose words carefully; be brief
• avoid hidden motives
• look for good behavior to comment upon
• follow through in the future (pp. 139-142).

In *Discipline with Dignity* (1988) Curwin and Mendler support using consequences in the classroom. For teachers, consequences work best when they are clear and specific and spelled out ahead of time. Predictability is important in helping students choose behavior.

Another tip is to have a range of alternatives. This gives the teacher discretion in matching consequences to situations. If accused of being unfair when applying different consequences for the same misbehavior, teachers can rely on the "fair is not always equal" principle. Teaching this concept first can prevent complaints later. Using the following example can help children understand this principle.

I have two children. One is a successful lawyer who makes $100,000 per year, but needs a $10,000 loan for a down payment on his dream house. My other child is a college dropout who has decided to go back to school and needs $10,000 for tuition. Who gets my only $10,000?

Most students will vote to give it to the second child. They see that different people have different needs, thus fair but not equal treatment is acceptable. Another quick example is to tell of the doctor who walked into his waiting room and said, "I'm going to dispense equal treatment today, giving all of you an aspirin." Equal, but is it fair?

After teaching this principle, the statement "I will be fair and I won't always be equal can serve as the teacher's guide for the year.

Creating effective consequences can be difficult for teachers, particularly if the teacher is accustomed to using punishment. A good start is to use the following four generic consequences for breaking any rule:

1. A reminder — restate the rule and tell the child that this is a reminder.

2. A warning — not a threat, but a stern warning that the behavior is contrary to the rule.

3. Develop an action plan in writing for improving the behavior. Restate the rule and put the responsibility on the child for correcting the problem.

4. Practice behavior. Role-playing new alternatives to old problem situations can help the child who lacks skills.

In recent years, Dinkmeyer (In Shiff, 1987) has continued to elaborate on using natural and logical consequences. Natural consequences require no arrangements by parents, and can be effective regardless of the child's goal. Logical consequences, because they are carefully structured by adults, are most effective for children whose goal is attention. If the child's goal is power or revenge, a logical consequence may seem like arbitrary punishment, particularly if the adult tries to administer it during the power struggle. Dinkmeyer suggests that for the child who uses arguing and tantrums to get his way, the logical consequence is to remove the opponent. If the adult can refuse to argue, walk away, and later try to work on the relationship with the child, chances for success are better. Consequences in general far more, effective when the relationship between child and adult is based on mutual respect and equality.

Another example can illustrate the division between consequences and punishment. Suppose Kenya forgets to take her homework to school. Mother finds it and brings it to school along with the admonition to "be more responsible" and "don't waste my time with your forgetfulness again." Is Mother's fussing and lecturing a natural or logical consequence? No, getting a zero on the homework until it was turned, in would be the logical consequence. All Mother has done is teach Kenya that she doesn't need to remember her homework, that Mother will bring it. The nagging only puts the focus on Kenya instead of the homework.

Would this example be different if Mother brings the homework with no critical remarks? Rescuing the child is still the result, even if the rescue is more pleasant. The only difference in the message is that forgetting homework is another way to gain Mother's attention. Responsibility for the homework gets lost in the emotions of dependence.

If the natural consequence for forgotten homework is a poor grade, are additional "consequences;" i.e., punishment, necessary? No. Kenya might be more afraid to forget her homework again, but punishment is still discouraging and can be damaging to self-esteem.

Do you let a child touch the proverbial hot stove as a natural consequence? Of course not. Consequences have to be structured in cases of potential harm. If Bernard can't stay out of the street, his mother cannot risk natural consequences, but must give him choices of other areas to play in, or he must play near the street only when supervised.

Encouragement Versus Praise

As documented previously, Dinkmeyer and associates have written extensively for parents and teachers, offering Adlerian methods for learning to guide young people into responsible choices. Closely related to natural and logical consequences is the Adlerian idea of encouragement versus praise. Encouragement helps children build self-confidence, and thus develop the courage to handle those times when .they are wrong and less than perfect. Encouraging adults accept children as they are and help them to believe in themselves. Recognition of effort and progress toward a goal are as important as the end product. Again, the difference is that of promoting the development of internal, as opposed to external, motivation. The best way to understand the difference between the two is to examine what we say.

Encouragement focuses on effort and improvement. "I see lots of improvement in the way you tackle those hard math problems." It's also important to acknowledge the child's strengths and contributions. "You're good at building models; I know you'll figure this one out." Appreciation and recognition go hand in hand to help the child gain confidence and perseverance. "I like the way you handled that." "It was thoughtful of you to help your little sister today." Avoiding the temptation to moralize may be difficult, but it can mean the difference between being encouraging or discouraging. "It looks like you really worked hard on that!" The previous statement is fine, but too many times we add, "Why can't you do that all the time?" Those additional words are very discouraging and present confusing messages to the child.

Praise teaches a child to conform, to please others, and to feel worthwhile only when getting ahead of others. "Good for you!" What about the others? Children may learn to fear disapproval or may stop contributing if not praised. "I'm so proud of you!" Is the message that I'm proud because you did it my way? Children may even become perfectionists, believing that they are worthwhile only when performing up to others' high standards. "You are certainly are an A + student." If

Praising a child who is discouraged and insecure may seem like a good way to motivate him, but the child generally feels unworthy of praise and frequently tries to prove that unworthiness. Another problem for the discouraged child is that he may feel like he can never earn praise again, so he sees no need in trying. "What a good job you did!" What if the child does not agree with your assessment? Whose evaluation is more important to nurture and refine? Praise can also be overused and become worthless through the repetition. How many times do teachers say "Good!" without giving more specific comments which would focus on the value of the work rather than the worker?

Pre-Packaged Programs/Resources

The contrasts are evident between the democratic Adlerian approaches and the autocratic methods of the past. No change is easy, and Dinkmeyer and other Adlerians offer many aids to parents and teachers who wish to become encouraging people in children's lives. Some of the Dinkmeyers' most popular programs include the *Systematic Training for Effective Parenting* (4th ed.), called the STEP series. Early Childhood STEP (1997) and the STEP/TEEN (1997), programs teach parents a variety of Adlerian skills. The Next STEP (1997) helps parents refine and sustain skills from the previous programs. A Spanish version is available as is a Biblical perspective version. Also available is New Beginnings (1987) which is for single parents and stepfamilies. Within the school setting, *Developing Understanding of Self and Others*, called DUSO (1982) is the very popular guidance program for elementary school classes. For over twenty years, Duso the Dolphin, and his friends have helped children understand their feelings and choices.

Applications in School and at Home

The use of consequences is a common thread among other writers interested in helping children develop responsibility for their own actions. Barbara Colorosa, a popular speaker and educator, uses a discipline cycle to assure that children's behavior is their responsibility whether at home or at school. The mother of six children, she uses natural and logical consequences extensively in her recommendations to parents and teachers. One of Colorosa's (1983, p. 3) clearest messages is "say what you mean, mean what you say, and do what you said you would do." Her attitude is positive and upbeat, full of humor and encouragement. She advises keeping discipline simple with a few meaningful rules and logical consequences for breaking those rules.

In her workshops, Colorosa often brings examples from her home. The age-old problem of getting your child to take out the garbage becomes a simple matter of following her insistence on consistency. If the child has gone to bed without taking out the garbage, she wakes him and with very little talking, focuses on remedying the situation, not the failures of the child.

With the current emphasis in schools on cooperative learning, some teachers report having problems with students wanting to work together on tests. A somewhat humorous and logical approach to cheating is to very calmly state that nothing is wrong with helping each other, but certainly the score should be split since more than one person obtained it. This is not retaliation in a punitive sense, but a logical result structured by the teacher.

Parent Effectiveness Training (1975) and *Teacher Effectiveness Training* (1977) are Thomas Gordon's contributions to developing self-discipline in children. His "No-Lose Method" involves parents and children in a mutual problem-solving process which leaves each party a winner. Democratic strategies include dividing household chores, negotiating routine rules, creating mutual respect, and generating concern for feelings. Assertive training is also a component, teaching that parents have needs and a right to meet those needs as well as the needs of their children. Parents are taught to be honest, assertive, and self-disclosing. These methods seek to modify children's behavior without demanding blind obedience to authority.

Being bothered while on the phone is an irritation felt by many parents. Most children are simply seeking attention, and their behavior will be made worse if ignored. Lashing out verbally or physically to get them to be quiet is also unproductive. Parents have the right to speak without interruption, but they must guide their children into honoring that right. The first time the phone problem occurs, the parent could take a moment to talk directly to the child, saying, "I know you want my attention right now, and I realize it may be important to you, but I have a call to complete. I will come get you when I am finished." If the problem continues to occur, then a problem-solving session needs to be planned with both sides contributing solutions that can be agreed to and written down if necessary.

William Glasser, also known for helping children see choices, continues to refine his original Reality Therapy (1965). As he develops the newer Control Theory (1984), consequences are called sanctions. Sanctions include the loss of freedom (go to your room) or a loss of privileges (no skateboarding) to be used as a last resort in changing misbehavior. He distinguishes between punishment and discipline, emphasizing that punished children feel a loss of control and power, and are not helped to learn that a better way of behaving is available. Calm negotiation of rules satisfies both the child's and adult's needs. Responsibility for creating a plan to change behavior is left with the child, but if the adult has to assist, Glasser is adamant that "what you do is as much *with* and as little *to* or *for* the child as possible" (1984, p. 200).

Choices are appropriate even for entire classes, Verble (1985) gives the example of the elementary class that as a whole dislikes math. Chances are that behavior will deteriorate during math class. Revising the curriculum is probably the best alternative, but for the moment, letting the class choose when to have math may alleviate a great deal of the behavior problem. Sharing the decision-making can be a very positive consequence far removed from punishment.

Verble also observes that many classes successfully plan consequences for routine behavior problems, but says that the teacher needs a plan for tackling those unexpected situations. She suggests a plan which begins with a question. For example, Felix blows up the class ant farm with a fire cracker. "How are you going to replace the ant farm?" The student has to see that his behavior is his problem, and that there is no question that he can correct the misbehavior. Felix is unable to think of ways to purchase a new ant farm, then the teacher makes helpful suggestions. "We've known for a long time that active students learn better than passive ones. The same is true in learning self-discipline" (p. 42).

Another advocate of building a child's feelings of self-worth and encouraging autonomy is Haim Ginott. His *Between Parent and Child* (1965) and *Teacher and Child* (1972) influenced another sizable group of parents and teachers hungry for alternatives to "spare the rod and spoil the child." Two of his followers, Adele Faber and Elaine Mazlish have successfully continued his work in their *Liberated Parents Liberated Children* (1974). Their parent workshops called "How to Talk So Kids Will Listen and Listen So Kids Will Talk" (1982) combine humor, emphasis on feelings, cooperation, and communication, with natural consequences forming an important component.

Those who may doubt that Adlerian techniques work with more serious misbehavior need only to read Nugent (1991), who reports a model juvenile justice program in California based on mutual respect, encouragement, goal-directed behavior, goal alignment, and social interest. Within that framework, Nelson's (1985) "3 R's" are followed in the use of logical consequences: they must be related, respectful, and reasonable. The program has operated since 1982 and approximately 600 youths have participated. The California Youth Authority recognized the model for its innovative programming, and effectiveness has been rated at 92 percent. Many of the consequences utilitized include community service work, restitution, educational tasks, career research, creative assignments, or counseling.

Another program for juvenile delinquents in Pensacola, Florida is the only one of ten similar programs in the United States to use

Adlerian techniques. Their non-punitive, encouraging approach also uses logical consequences. In reporting their procedures, Hirschorn (1982) points out that with rebellious adolescents, logical consequences may not be quite as effective as a problem-solving staff/student meeting. At this meeting, both sides brainstorm until satisfactory results have been achieved. Using recidivism as the measure, initial success rates were over 85 percent.

SUMMARY

Wright (1982) has used consequences extensively in his private practice and offers this summary. Regardless of the target population, natural logical consequences can work only if the parent or teacher is patient, matter-of-fact, friendly, and willing to accept a child's choice. Logical consequences are not to be viewed as an end in themselves, but as strategies for getting youngsters to reevaluate their behavior and to investigate possibilities. Understanding, the reasons for the behavior and why it has caused problems must also accompany the use of consequences. As Dinkmeyer and McKay (1997) gently remind us, "patience plus practice equals progress" (p. 80).

REFERENCES

Adler, A. (1963). *The problem child.* New York: Capricorn.

Colorosa, B. (1983). *Discipline: Winning at teaching..* Boulder, CO: Media for Kids.

Colorosa, B. (1983). *Discipline: Winning at teaching without beating your kids* (cassette tape series). Boulder, CO: Media for Kids.

Curwin, R., & Mendler, A. (1988). *Discipline with dignity.* Alexandria, VA: Association for Supervision and Curriculum Development.

Dinkmeyer, D. and McKay, G. (1997). *The parent's guide.* (STEP/Teen) Circle Pines, MN: American Guidance Service.

Dinkmeyer, D. (1965). *Child development.* Englewood Cliffs, NJ: Prentice Hall.

Dinkmeyer, D., and Dreikurs, R. (1963). *Encouraging children to learn: The encouragement process.* Englewood Cliffs, NJ: Prentice Hall.

Dinkmeyer, D., McKay, G., and McKay, J. (1987). *New beginnings.* Champaign, IL: Research Press.

Dinkmeyer, D., McKay, G., Dinkmeyer, D. Jr., Dinkmeyer, J., & McKay, J. (1987). *The effective parent.* Circle Pines, MN: American Guidance Service.

Dinkmeyer, D., & McKay, G., (1997). *The parent's handbook* (4th ed. of STEP). Circle Pines, MN: American Guidance Service.

Dinkmeyer, D., Sr., & Dinkmeyer, D., Jr. (1982). *DUSO: Developing Understanding of Self and Others* [Kit]. Circle Pines, MN: American Guidance Service.

Dinkmeyer, D. (1987). Teaching responsibility. In E. Shiff (Ed.), *Experts advise parents* (pp.171-195). New York: Delacorte Press.

Dreikurs, R. with Soltz, V. (1964). *Children: The challenge.* New York: Hawthorne Books.

Dreikurs, R. (1968). *Psychology in the classroom* (2n ed.). New

York: Harper & Row.

Dreikurs, R., Grunwald, B., & Pepper, F. (1971). *Maintaining sanity in the classroom*. New York: Harper &,Row.

Dreikurs, R, & Cassel, P. (1974). *Discipline without tears*. New York: Hawthorp Books, Inc.

Faber, A. & Mazlish, E. (1980). *How to talk so kids will listen & listen so kids will talk*. New York: Avon Books.

Faber, A. & Mazlish, E. (1974). *Liberated parents liberated children*. New York: Avon Books.

Ginott, H. (1965). *Between parent and child*. New York: Avon Books.

Ginott, H. (1972). *Teacher and child*. New York: Avon Books.

Glasser, W. (1984). *Control theory*. New York: Harper & Row.

Glasser, W. (1965). *Reality therapy*. New York: Harper & Row.

Gordon, T. (1981). Crippling our children with discipline. *Journal of Education, 3,* 228-243.

Gordon, T. (1975). *Parent effectiveness training*. New York: New American Library.

Gordon, T. (1977). *Teacher effectiveness training*. New York: David McKay.

Hirschorn, S. (1982). Pensacola new pride: An Adlerian-based alternative for juvenile delinquents. *Individual Psychology, 48,* 129-137.

Hyman, I., McDowell, E., & Raines, B. (1975). Corporal punishment and alternatives in schools. *Inequality in Education, 23,*5-20.

Martin, B. (1975). Parent child relationships. In F. Horowitz (Ed.) *Review of Child Development Research, 4.* Chicago: University of Chicago Press.

Nelsog, J. (1985). The three R's of logical consequences, the three R's of punishment, and the six steps for winning children over. *Individual Psychology, 41,*161-165.

Nugent, L. (1991). A model juvenile justice program. *Individual Psychology, 47,* 189-198.

Verble, M.(1985). How to encourage self-discipline. *Learning, 14,* 40,41.

Wright, L. (1982). The use of logical consequences in counseling children. *School Counselor, 30,* 37-49.

Name Index

SUBJECT INDEX